Deformed FROGS
A Cause and Effect Investigation

by Kathy Allen

WITHDRAWN

Consultant:
Michael J. Lannoo, PhD
Author of *Malformed Frogs: The Collapse of Aquatic Ecosystems*
Professor of Anatomy and Cell Biology
Indiana University School of Medicine
Indianapolis, Indiana

CAPSTONE PRESS
a capstone imprint

Fact Finders are published by Capstone Press,
151 Good Counsel Drive, P.O. Box 669, Mankato, Minnesota 56002.
www.capstonepub.com

032010
005740CGF10

Books published by Capstone Press are manufactured with paper
containing at least 10 percent post-consumer waste.

Library of Congress Cataloging-in-Publication Data

Allen, Kathy.
  Deformed frogs : a cause and effect investigation / by Kathy Allen.
     p. cm. — (Fact finders. animals on the edge)
  Includes bibliographical references and index.
  Summary: "Describes the cause and effect of deformed frogs in the wild"—Provided by publisher.
  ISBN 978-1-4296-4533-1 (library binding)
  1. Frogs—Effect of pollution on—Juvenile literature. 2. Frogs—Diseases—Genetic aspects—Juvenile
literature. 3. Frogs—Conservation—Juvenile literature. I. Title. II. Series.

  QL668.E2A453 2011
  597.8'921727—dc22   2010004412

Editorial Credits
Marissa Bolte, editor; Ashlee Suker, designer; Kelly Garvin, media researcher;
     Eric Manske, production specialist.

Photo Credits
AP Images/Minnesota Pollution Control Agency, 10 (top); Craig Line, 5
Corbis/Brooks Craft, 25; Karl Ammann, 26
Dreamstime/Belliot, 16; Jurrie Torn, 9; Paul Wolf, 11
Dwight R. Kuhn, cover, 4, 10 (bottom)
Fotolia/ChaoticMind, 6
Getty Images, Inc., 21; Photolibrary/Wendy Shattil and Bob Rozinski, 13; Taxi/F Millington, 17;
     Visuals Unlimited/Glenn Olivier, 10 (middle), Gary Meszaros, 27
Michael J. Lannoo, 22, 24
Michael Redmer, 18
Shutterstock/Lori Howard; Marina Strizhak, design elements
Visuals Unlimited/Biodisc, 23; Joe McDonald, 14

TABLE OF CONTENTS

CHAPTER 1

Freaky Frogs

Students on a summer field trip found something odd in a Minnesota pond. As they walked, they saw hundreds of frogs jumping at their feet. That was normal. Frogs are easy to find in the middle of summer. But some frogs were having a hard time jumping. Something was wrong with them. Many had twisted legs. Others had extra legs or were missing legs.

At first the students thought that the frogs they found had broken legs. Then they looked more closely.

Freaky frogs aren't an unusual sight. Normally between 1 to 2 percent of frog populations have some sort of flaw. But the frogs found in Minnesota were different. Some sites had as many as 60 percent of frogs with something wrong with them. Soon after the discovery in Minnesota, more strange frogs were found in Canada.

There are more than 3,500 different kinds of frogs and toads.

Today deformed frogs have been found in at least 38 U.S. states. They have also been found around the world. Experts have never seen so many strange frogs before. Scientists are more than curious about these frogs—they are worried.

Frog Distribution

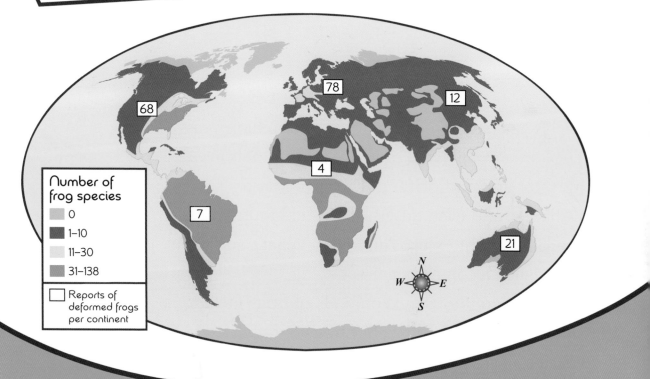

Number of frog species

- 0
- 1–10
- 11–30
- 31–138

Reports of deformed frogs per continent

68
78
12
4
7
21

N W E S

Disappearing Frogs

Frogs with odd numbers of legs are not the only thing to worry about. Fewer frogs live on Earth because their habitat is disappearing. Although frogs live almost everywhere, they like wet places best. But humans build on wetlands. Ponds and marshes are drained to build homes and shopping malls. Some species of frogs have disappeared completely. For example, the golden toad in Costa Rica and the gastric brooding frog in Australia are extinct.

species—a group of animals with similar features

extinct—no longer living; an extinct animal is one that has died out with no more of its kind

Frogs have been around for 200 million years. They are amphibians. They live part of their lives in water and part on land. They live in forests, wetlands, and even deserts. Frogs are found on every continent except Antarctica. What's so special about such a common animal?

There are thousands of kinds of frogs in various shapes, sizes, and colors. But frogs of different species all share one thing in common—they have thin skin. Their skin soaks up the sunlight, air, and water around them. If something changes in a frog's habitat, the frogs change with it.

You may wonder why we should be worried about what happens to frogs. People aren't frogs. Something that hurts frogs may not harm humans. But frogs are like humans in a very important way.

Normal Frog Characteristics

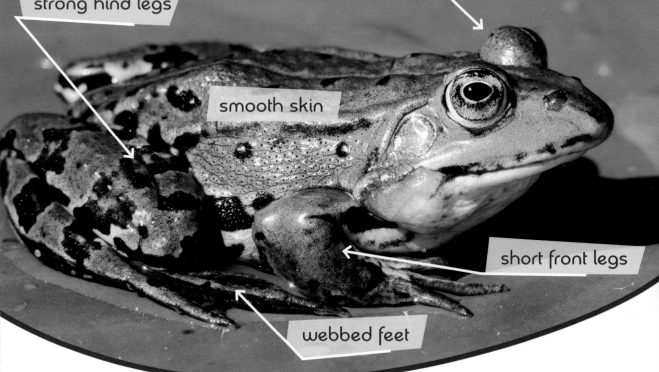

round, bulging eyes

strong hind legs

smooth skin

short front legs

webbed feet

Like humans, frogs are vertebrates, which means they have a spine. Their limbs are also very similar to human limbs. The upper part of the limb has one long bone. The lower part has two bones that attach to the wrist or ankle and hand or foot. Scientists fear that whatever is causing deformities in frogs could someday do the same to humans. Is there something in the water, they wonder, that could be the cause?

Deformed Frog Characteristics

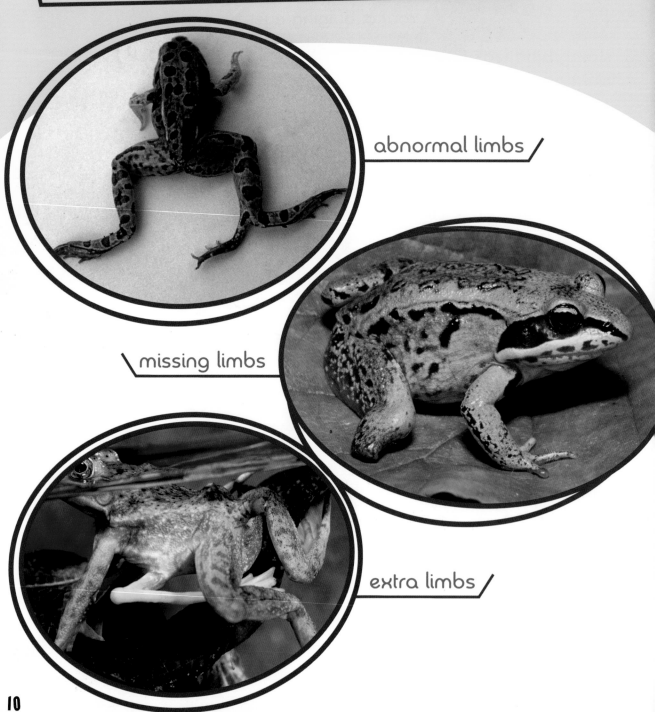

abnormal limbs

missing limbs

extra limbs

Snakes are one of the frog's main predators.

Scientists found that all the deformed frogs they studied were young. A frog with twisted or extra legs will not be able to reach adulthood. With bent or missing legs, a frog cannot escape predators.

Scientists also believe that these frogs may be smaller and weaker. This condition may make it hard for frogs to survive cold, harsh weather. Healthy frogs dig burrows to stay warm and safe. An imperfect frog would have a harder time making a burrow and keeping out of the cold.

WHAT COULD BE CAUSING DEFORMED FROGS?

CHAPTER 2

Many Theories

When students found deformed frogs in 1995, scientists tried not to jump to conclusions. They wanted to learn more about the frogs' conditions first. But then more funny-looking frogs were reported across the United States. People started thinking of **theories** to explain the problem. Some researchers wondered if they were finding more of these frogs because they were looking more closely for them. They noted that frogs with unusual body parts had been seen in the past. Deformed frogs were recorded as early as 1706.

Frogs have been around a long time. Scientists thought that these changes could happen naturally over time. Natural changes in frog populations could include extra legs or eyes. Others thought that frogs were missing legs because of predators. They believed birds and fish had taken bites out of the young frogs.

theory—an idea that explains something that is unknown

Scientists had many theories about what could be causing frog deformities.

Beginning in the 1950s, scientists noted more deformed frog sightings. In the last 10 years, the number of deformed frogs has gone up. In some places, the increase has been as much as 30 percent.

But if there is a natural cause for twisted and missing frog legs, why do reports of them seem to be increasing? Why are so many frogs being found now with weird-looking body parts? Some people thought that predators might be the cause. But most of the shortened legs have no scars. Frogs sit with their legs tucked underneath their bodies. This position makes it hard for predators to damage only the frogs' legs.

Only a few predators could cause this kind of damage. Dragonfly nymphs bite legs off tadpoles. Water turtles prey on grown frogs from below, hoping to grab them by the legs. But such a small number of hunters wouldn't be able to cause the amount of damage scientists were seeing.

Finally, scientists realized that even frogs in areas without predators had missing limbs. Scientists came to think that something went wrong as these frogs grew.

Deformed frogs are easier for predators to catch.

Pesticides have already been found to be harmful to frogs and other living things.

If the cause wasn't predators, what else could it be? Could chemicals in the water affect growing frogs? There are plenty of chemicals to choose from.

Each year farmers in the United States use more than 1 billion pounds (454 million kilograms) of **pesticides**. These chemicals kill bugs and pests that attack crops. Pesticides can also seep into groundwater or travel through the air to nearby ponds. Some reports have found deformed frogs on or near farms but not in the surrounding areas. A frog's thin skin could absorb chemicals in the water into their own bodies. Scientists wondered if there was something deadly in the groundwater.

pesticide—a chemical used to kill insects and other pests that eat crops

The Life of a Frog

To understand why chemicals could cause frogs to grow in strange ways, it helps to know about a frog's life cycle. Frogs spend much of their lives in water. Different kinds of frogs have different life cycles, but a normal frog's life cycle has the same stages. A female frog lays eggs in a pond or stream. Then the male fertilizes the eggs.

From birth, a frog's life is a wet one. The eggs hatch into tadpoles. The tadpoles use their tails to swim until their legs grow. After that, they lose their tails. These new frogs spend the rest of their lives moving between land and water.

Scientists discovered that flatworm cysts caused the growth of as many as 10 extra limbs.

Polluted water isn't the only theory scientists have. Scientists believe that the flatworm **parasite** could be a cause. Flatworms attack tadpoles, which create **cysts** in the tadpoles' limb buds. These cysts trick the body into growing extra limbs. To test their theory, scientists planted little beads into tadpoles. They wanted to learn if the beads acted like cysts. The scientists hoped to recreate the damage the worm could do. Sure enough, many of those frogs grew extra legs.

parasite—an animal or plant that lives on or inside another animal or plant

cyst—an abnormal sac on the inside or outside of the body

But the experiment didn't answer the mystery of the missing legs. Some scientists blame ultraviolet (UV) rays. UV-B light is dangerous to humans and animals. A part of Earth's atmosphere, called the **ozone layer**, protects living things from UV-B. But chemicals in refrigerators, air conditioners, and hairspray have damaged the ozone. Those chemicals are now banned, but nothing can fix the damage already done. Imagine those frog eggs floating on top of a lake. Floating at the water's surface, the eggs easily soak up the sun. If UV-B is causing defects, it would explain why so many abnormal frogs are being found now.

HOW DO DEFORMED FROGS AFFECT THE ECOSYSTEM?

ozone layer—the thin layer of gas high above Earth's surface that blocks out some of the Sun's harmful rays

CHAPTER 3

Many Answers

Scientists are working hard to figure out what's causing deformities in frogs. They think frogs reflect early changes to their habitat. With their thin skin, frogs are very sensitive to their environment. And frogs are a vital part of the ecosystem in which they live. An ecosystem is a complex collection of living and nonliving things. When one piece of the puzzle is missing, it affects all the other pieces.

Frogs are different from humans. What harms a frog does not necessarily harm a human. But frogs soak in the same water that humans drink. They breathe the same air that humans breathe. Humans are affected by changes around them, just like other animals.

Abnormal limbs are a common problem in vertebrates.

Scientists found that chemicals in the water, parasites, and UV-B rays could all be causing defects in frogs. But each of them can affect frog populations in various places. It became clear that there could be more than one right answer. In the end, scientists had a list of at least 25 different ideas. Their ideas included both natural and man-made causes.

Finding answers often leads to more questions. Lab tests showed that chemicals could kill frogs. But frogs raised in a laboratory live in a controlled environment. Their world is much different from frogs that live in the wild. These tests also showed that parasites could cause frogs to grow extra legs. But what about all the frogs with missing legs? If UV-B rays are causing deformities, why don't the rays affect all frogs? After all, no frog can survive without light.

Scientists wonder what deformed frogs may mean to humans.

Parasites are only one piece of the deformed frog puzzle.

If parasites could be the problem, then doesn't that mean that pollution isn't? Not necessarily. Scientists realized that chemicals from nearby farms could cause extra nutrients to grow in the water. The extra nutrients could lead to more snails living in the water. Young flatworm parasites use snails as a host. The more snails, the more hosts for the flatworms. When the flatworms reach their next life stage, they move onto tadpoles. The mystery of deformed frogs could be solved by both answers— parasites and pollution.

COULD THE CAUSES BEHIND DEFORMED FROGS ALSO AFFECT PEOPLE?

CHAPTER 4

Protecting Frogs

Today scientists, animal lovers, farmers, and gardeners work to protect frogs. They have started to protect the frog's habitat. Many wetlands have been preserved and protected so wildlife can live there undisturbed. ATVs and other off-road vehicles can tear through a frog habitat in just seconds. These vehicles have been banned in some areas.

Some conservation groups have started captive breeding programs to restock wild populations. Others are simply trying to educate people on the risks frogs are facing.

Many groups are trying to spread the word about frogs in trouble.

One of the best ways to protect frogs is to take care of the water. Keeping water free of chemicals and pesticides is a way to keep frog habitats safe. Farmers take extra care when using pesticides. Water treatment plants can take measures to reduce pesticide levels in water. Buying organic food discourages farmers from using pesticides at all. If their watery world is safe, frogs are safe. In a clean home, these familiar and amazing creatures can get back to the important work they do.

The loss of frogs would create a problem for animals that depend on frogs for food.

Frogs are important to their ecosystems. They hunt insects that may annoy people. And in turn, frogs are a food source for meat eaters. A frog spends its day hunting insects. A predator such as a hedgehog that eats a frog gets everything it needs in one gulp.

And consider the frog you might find in your garden. That frog eats bugs and pests that could be feasting on your garden plants. Farmers also like frogs because they eat pests that can be harmful to valuable crops.

Frogs may not be cute and cuddly, but protecting them protects all the other animals in their ecosystem. The deformed frogs shine a light on just how important these critters are.

Frog Ecosystems

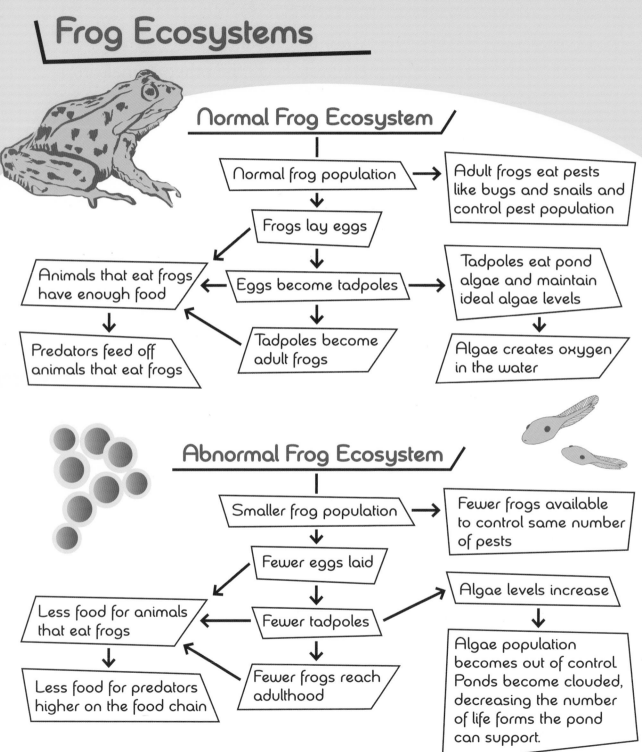

Normal Frog Ecosystem

Normal frog population → Adult frogs eat pests like bugs and snails and control pest population

Frogs lay eggs

Eggs become tadpoles → Tadpoles eat pond algae and maintain ideal algae levels

Animals that eat frogs have enough food

Tadpoles become adult frogs

Algae creates oxygen in the water

Predators feed off animals that eat frogs

Abnormal Frog Ecosystem

Smaller frog population → Fewer frogs available to control same number of pests

Fewer eggs laid

Fewer tadpoles → Algae levels increase

Less food for animals that eat frogs

Fewer frogs reach adulthood

Algae population becomes out of control Ponds become clouded, decreasing the number of life forms the pond can support.

Less food for predators higher on the food chain

RESOURCES TO HELP FROGS

THE AMPHIBIAN ARK

The goal of the Amphibian Ark is to keep amphibians safe in their own environments. Scientists at the Ark believe that working to restore natural habitats and current populations is the first step to help amphibians around the world.

NATIONAL WILDLIFE FEDERATION

With more than 4 million supporters, the National Wildlife Federation aims to be the voice for wildlife conservation. Their goal is to make sure that future generations have the opportunity to explore the natural world.

NORTH AMERICAN AMPHIBIAN MONITORING PROGRAM

Founded in 1995, the North American Amphibian Monitoring Program watches breeding population levels of frogs and toads throughout Mexico, the United States, and Canada. Volunteers are asked to track local amphibians through each species' unique vocal calls.

SAVE THE FROGS

Save the Frogs is a nonprofit organization that helps protect amphibian populations all over the world. The group hopes to increase the amount of funding scientists receive for researching threatened species. They also work to educate people about how to respect and appreciate wildlife.

Glossary

cyst (SIST)—an abnormal sac on the inside or outside of the body

extinct (ek-STINGKT)—no longer living; an extinct animal is one that has died out with no more of its kind

nutrient (NOO-tree-uhnt)—something that is needed by people, animals, or plants for life and growth

ozone layer (OH-zohn LAY-ur)—the thin layer of gases high above Earth's surface that blocks out some of the Sun's harmful rays

parasite (PAIR-uh-site)—an animal or plant that lives on or inside another animal or plant

pesticide (PESS-tuh-side)—a chemical used to kill insects and other pests that eat crops

species (SPEE-sheez)—a group of animals with similar features

theory (THEE-ur-ee)—an idea that explains something that is unknown

wetland (WET-land)—an area of land covered by water and plants; marshes, swamps, and bogs are wetlands

Read More

Hamilton, Garry. *Frog Rescue: Changing the Future for Endangered Wildlife.* Buffalo, N.Y.: Firefly Books, 2004.

Turner, Pamela S. *The Frog Scientist.* Scientists in the Field. Boston: Houghton Mifflin Books for Children, 2009.

Whiting, Jim. *Frogs in Danger.* A Robbie Reader. Hockessin, Del.: Mitchell Lane Publishers, 2008.

Internet Sites

FactHound offers a safe, fun way to find Internet sites related to this book. All of the sites on FactHound have been researched by our staff.

Here's all you do:

Visit *www.facthound.com*

FactHound will fetch the best sites for you!

Index